# Cooperation:
## Learning through Laughter
## Second Edition

### 51 Brief Activities for
### Groups of All Ages

by
Charlene C. Wenc

Illustrated by Sally Kremer
Introduction by Eleanor Lawrence

Copyright 1993
by Charlene C. Wenc

ISBN 0-932796-51-6

Library of Congress Catalog Number 92-83883

Printed in the United States of America
First printing, 1986

Current printing of the second edition (last digit):
9 8 7 6 5 4 3 2 1

Publisher—
**Educational Media Corporation®**
P.O. Box 21311
Minneapolis, MN 55421
(612) 781-0088

Production editor—
**Don L. Sorenson**

Graphic design—
**Earl R. Sorenson**

Cover Illustration—
**David Anderson, Cropmark Services, Inc.**

**This book is dedicated to
the children of Brook Forest School
Oak Brook, Illinois**

## MY SCHOOL

My school, my school
Is very cool. It never has a frown
Nor puts someone down
Because it is my school!

*Erin Sorvillo*

Fourth Grade Student
Brook Forest School

## Acknowledgments

To my husband, Steve,
for his love and encouragement.

To the wonderful teachers of Brook Forest School
for their inspiration and help.

To my sons, Stephen and Matthew,
for their enthusiasm.

To my fellow Adlerians who taught me cooperation.

# Table of Contents

## LIST OF ILLUSTRATIONS

Charlene C. Wenc

# Introduction

As a classroom teacher, each Fall you face a new group of twenty to thirty individuals entrusted to your care for an adventure in learning.

Each teacher hopes that, as the year progresses, these individuals will develop a cohesiveness with one another—a group identity—where caring and mutual support are the order of the day. If students and teacher succeed, the classroom is transformed into an encouraging emotional environment providing a fertile ground for the educational experience.

Too often, though, teachers think they can only provide an opportunity to learn subject-matter material, feeling that they have little or no control or influence over the classroom's emotional climate. If you are like many teachers, you have an intense concern for your classroom's atmosphere, but find little emphasis on how to create and maintain an environment in which children can work together effectively.

My colleague, Charlene Wenc (author of the present book), and I began looking for the "magic" ingredient that was *present* in the cohesive classroom that was *missing* in other classrooms. Obviously, it isn't possible to isolate any one factor and say, "This is it! As long as we do this, we'll succeed!" However, we found that the classroom that seems to provide a strong, supportive, concerned base for its students is the classroom where members exhibit the ability to work together for mutual benefit, the classroom where students have learned *the art of cooperation.*

Psychologist Alfred Adler stressed the importance of cooperation in his concept of *social interest.* For Adler, social interest includes the ability to "see with the eyes of another, hear with the ears of another, and feel with the heart of another." Adlerian Rudolf Dreikurs called social interest "the expression of our capacity to give and take." According to author Edith A. Dewey[1] social interest includes participation, contribution, involvement, mutual respect, a sense of belonging, of focusing on the task (instead of seeking reward or praise), and of cooperation. Adler saw social interest as an *inherent capacity* in all human beings, but one which must be *developed.*

Assuming that the classroom's atmosphere is not solely the responsibility of the teacher, but the responsibility of everyone in the class, emphasis should be on helping one another rather than competing with one another. To quote Dreikurs, "When we become more invested in group dynamics and achievements—rather than our own recognition and achievement—cooperation is obtained."

Cooperation is a public act. Group members taking cooperative actions risk the possibility that others will see them making a mistake. In our society, many view *mistakes* as *failures*. Strong competitors find the risk of making a mistake among others unthinkable; strong cooperators, on the other hand, realize that when all benefit, they also benefit, and that all can benefit even from a mistake. Working together teaches children to find satisfaction in group support and approval (as well as in their private activities).

In identifying cooperation as the "magic" ingredient in the cohesive classroom, we recognize that what appears to be "magic" is really the result of intention, planning, organization, preparation, and plain hard work.

After hearing Adlerian counselor and educator Marie Hartwell-Walker speak on techniques of encouragement and cooperation, we began to develop concrete ways to show children the power and beauty of cooperation. As elementary school counselors, we started by giving students a few guidance activities emphasizing cooperation. We were pleased with the immediate results of these efforts, and were encouraged to develop our ideas more fully. The outcome was a guidance curriculum composed of a collection of activities designed to provide groups with the opportunity to experience cooperation. These activities are gathered together in this book.

We found in using the curriculum that for some students the hardest part of cooperation is giving up their desire for control; for others, it is difficult to share or to listen. As cooperation develops, students find joy in sharing, in listening, and in the realization that another's ideas may be as good as—or even better than—their own, and so are able to accept others' ideas in group living. Benefits of the "cooperation curriculum" come not only in carrying out the activities, but also in referring back to the activities at those times when cooperation is *lacking* in the group.

Charlene C. Wenc

Teachers and other group leaders may choose from among these activities those which will appeal to their particular groups, and may use them on whatever schedule they wish. We encourage you to use them often—we know from experience that they work in building group cohesiveness. To illustrate their success, we'd like to tell you a story:

## "Don't Let Go of the Rope"

Several years ago when Amtrak was in its heyday, a kindergarten class took the train from Kalamazoo to Battle Creek, Michigan, to tour the Kellogg factory.

The children boarded a school bus to be taken to the train station where they boarded the Amtrak. Upon arrival in Battle Creek, they were met by their bus and were taken to the factory.

The tour of the factory was well organized, not too long, and was followed by an ice-cream and cereal treat provided by Kellogg. After this, the children rode the school bus back to their school.

One little girl arrived home from the tour to find her grand-mother waiting to hear about the trip. Before they got into great detail about the day, the grandmother asked, "Where is your Mom? Didn't she go with you? Isn't she one of the room mothers?"

The little girl answered, "Yes," her mom was one of the room mothers, but she had not gone on the trip. The grandmother asked which mothers had accompanied the class. To this the little girl responded that NO room mothers had gone with the class. Knowing the difficulties involved in corralling thirty 5-year-olds, the grandmother was aghast. How could a responsible adult possibly go on an all-day field trip without any assistance?

To this the little girl responded, "All Miss Jones said was we can have a good time today all on our own—just 'DON'T LET GO OF THE ROPE.' "

*Eleanor Lawrence*
Kansas City, Missouri

[1]Edith A. Dewey. *Basic Applications of Adlerian Psychology.* Coral Spring, FL: CMTI Press, 1978.

# COOPERATION:
## Learning through Laughter
## Second Edition

## 51 Brief Activities for
## Groups of All Ages

# Part I
# Cooperation Builds Group Cohesiveness

Group Web

Charlene C. Wenc

Activity 1
# A Bag Full of Cooperation

## Purpose

To stress mutual respect and cooperation.

## Materials

Four or five grocery bags with four or five items in each (Example: cup, hat, keys, ruler, sponge, tray, blocks, gloves, scarf)

## Procedure

1. Divide the class into four or five groups.
2. Each group is given one bag of props.
3. Tell the group that their job is to create a short skit using all props and to be certain everyone has a part.
4. The groups are given five minutes to plan their skits.
5. Each group then presents their skit to the rest of the class.

## Suggestions for Discussion

How did you feel during your skit?

Why was your group able to work together?

How did it feel to have a part in this activity?

Why was the audience important?

**Ball Toss**

Charlene C. Wenc

Activity 2

# Ball Toss

## Purpose

To show that everyone needs to feel included to have a cooperative group.

## Materials

One large rubber ball

## Procedure

1. Have the class form a circle.
2. Tell them that *without speaking* to one another, they are to toss the ball across the circle to see how long it takes for everyone to have a turn to catch and pass it.
3. They must pay attention to who has the ball.
4. Do this *one* time.
5. Next time, tell the class that they can *toss* the ball, but they may not *catch* it again if they have already caught it one time.
6. You are part of the circle. Stop the game after two or three minutes each time.

## Suggestions for Discussion

Why does everyone want to be part of the group?

What does it feel like to be left out?

What can we do to include everyone in our class?

Activity 3

# Beat the Cooperative Clock

Purpose

To make a cooperative effort to include everyone in a group.

## Materials

One soft ball

## Procedure

1. Have the class form a circle.
2. Tell them the task is to see how fast they can toss the ball to each person in the group at least one time.
3. It is important to pay attention to who has and has not had the ball in order to complete the activity.
4. Tell them you are going to time them. Ready! Go!
5. Tell the class the time they took and ask if they want to try to beat it.
6. Play again if they wish.

## Suggestions for Discussion

How were you able to go so fast?

Was it hard to include everyone?

How does it feel to be included in a group?

Let's remember that good feeling and include everyone today!

Charlene C. Wenc

Activity 4

# Changing Groups

## Purpose

To emphasize that cooperation doesn't only take place with good friends; our group can include many different people, not just the ones we are with normally.

## Materials

None

## Procedure

1. Tell the class this game is about making many different kinds of groups.
2. Flick the lights on and off to stop the action. Tell the class that when you flick the lights, they should stop to listen to directions for forming the next group.
3. Below are some of the different groups the class can make:
   a. Group of two
   b. Group of three
   c. Group of four—everyone with the same color on
   d. Group of five—everyone with the same size nose
   e. Group of two—make the number four with your bodies on the floor
   f. Group of one—ask them to return to their seats

## Suggestions for Discussion

How did you cooperate in this game?

Were you with people you always play with? (Sometimes you have to cooperate with strangers or people you don't know very well.)

What would happen in our room if we only cooperated with our best friends?

Activity 5
# Cooperative Hands
# Around the Room

## Purpose

To create a visual record of the cooperative actions of the children.

## Materials

Make copies of the shape of a hand and place the copies on a shelf in the classroom. Next to them, place a box for the "filled-in" hands.

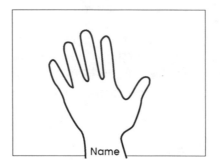

## Procedure

1. Tell the children that the "hands" are to be used to record any cooperative act that they themselves do and wish to record.
2. Tell them to get a "hand," write their name on it, and write down their cooperative act.
3. They are then to cut out the "hand" and place it in the box and you will add it to a "Hands Around the Room" display.

## Suggestions for Discussion

What kinds of things could we include in this activity?

How many think they can fill in two hands today?

Charlene C. Wenc

Activity 6
# Cooperative Pictures

## Purpose
To show children that cooperation can be fun.

## Materials
Drawing paper and one crayon per child

## Procedure
1. Tell the children that you are going to draw a picture together.
2. Ask the children to write their names on their papers, then to turn their papers over.
3. Now tell the class to close their eyes and draw the outline of a house (without any windows or doors).
4. Ask them to open their eyes and to pass their papers to the person next to them.
5. Follow this same procedure, asking the class to draw:
   a. windows and a door
   b. a sun in the sky
   c. a fence
   d. flowers
   e. a car or a pig in the yard

**Note:** These pictures can be part of a bulletin board or hall display.

## Suggestions for Discussion
Did you have fun?

Can cooperation be fun?

Is cooperation necessary? Why?

Activity 7
# Find Out Who

## Purpose
To build group cohesiveness.

## Materials
Ditto sheet for each student and the teacher. Example:
Find out who . . .
1. Has the same shoes on as you
2. Likes the same T.V. show as you
3. Likes the same subject in school as you
4. Lives the closest to your house
5. Has as many brothers and sisters as you
6. Plays the same sport as you
7. Has the same color eyes as you
8. Has been to your favorite place

## Procedure
1. Ask each child to take out a pencil.
2. Tell them this is a detective game in which they will find the answers by interviewing others in the group.
3. Hand out the sheets. Go over them with the younger children.
4. Tell them to answer each item with a group member's name.

**Note:** Items on the list can be changed to fit your group better or to repeat the activity.

## Suggestions for Discussion
What is something new you discovered about someone in our class?

How did this activity take cooperation?

Activity 8
# Find the Pennies

## Purpose

To develop cooperation and concentration among group members.

## Materials

Eight to ten pennies

## Procedure

1. The class stands in a tight circle.
2. Three people are selected to be "finders," who go to the center of the circle, sit down, and close their eyes.
3. Pass pennies to the children next to you.
4. The children in the circle hold their hands out in front of themselves, passing the pennies around the circle until you say "Stop."
5. When you say stop, the children in the circle close their hands. The finders open their eyes, and each has two guesses as to which children have pennies.
6. If a finder guesses correctly, the person caught replaces the finder in the center of the circle.

## Suggestions for Discussion

How did we cooperate in this activity?

How did you feel about being a finder?

About being a member of the circle?

Activity 9
# Group Web

## Purpose
To foster the concept that things in a group are better for all when cooperation exists.

## Materials
Three or four large balls of yarn in various colors

## Procedure
1. The class sits in a tight circle on the floor.
2. The teacher starts by throwing one of the yarn balls across the circle to someone on the other side, holding onto the end so that the yarn unwinds as it goes.
3. The person receiving the ball throws it on, keeping the strand so that the continuous path of the ball can be traced.
4. This will happen spontaneously, and the fewer directions you give the better.
5. When the first ball is well on its way, start a second, and then a third, and perhaps a fourth, so that the circle becomes a webbing of yarn.
6. The group is told to hold the yarn tightly, then to carefully let it down, and to loosen it. Ask them which they liked best.
7. The participants will say they like it better when they are holding the web tightly. Ask how the group helps to make the web beautiful. Cooperation is stressed here.

## Note:
a. Once the web is completed, the group may crawl under it, hang it on the wall, or suspend it from the ceiling.
b. The class is usually thrilled with their creation and seems to enjoy keeping it for a while.

## Suggestions for Discussion
Ideas for discussion are included in the directions.

It is important to ask the questions as they are included in the activity.

Charlene C. Wenc

# Part II
# Cooperation is Working Together

**Book Balance**

Activity 10
# Alphabet Race

## Purpose

To work together and to treat our teammates well.

## Materials

Chalkboard

Chalk

## Procedure

1. Divide the group into three teams.
2. Line up each group, in relay order, in front of the chalkboard; provide a piece of chalk for each team.
3. Tell the group that we are going to write the alphabet on the board.
4. Each team member is to write only one letter; the next member writes the *next* letter in order. (Example: first, A; second, B; third, C.) Keep going until you have finished the alphabet.
5. The first team finished is the winning team.

## Suggestions for Discussion

What did people say to you when you were on the team that encouraged you? That discouraged you?

Do most people try their hardest when they are on a team? What does "their hardest" mean? (In a classroom, children volunteer more readily when a question is general in nature. They will risk giving information when it doesn't apply just to them.)

How do you like people to treat you when you are on their team?

Are teams always fair? What can you do when they are not?

Activity 11
# "Blind Man's" Cooperative Walk

## Purpose

To allow the class to experience working together and to experience the importance of trust.

## Materials

Blindfolds for half of the class

## Procedure

1. Divide the class into partners.
2. Tell them to decide who will go first. (This is an interesting process to observe. If necessary, limit time to fifteen seconds for this choice to be made).
3. The person to go first will be given the blindfold to put on.
4. Tell the class that they are to take their partners on a "Blind Man's" Cooperative Walk around the room. Their responsibility is to protect their Blind Man from any danger. Ready? Go! Give them just a few minutes.
5. Reverse the roles for the next walk.

**Note:** Some groups, after a few turns around the room, can be moved to the hallway or playground areas.

## Suggestions for Discussion

How did it feel to be blind? What was the hardest part of this activity?

Did you learn anything in this activity that could help you this coming week?

Activity 12
# Book Balance

## Purpose

To experience working together and to see the importance of planning together.

## Materials

Two hardcover books (size of encyclopedia volumes)

## Procedure

1. Divide the class into partners.
2. Tell the group the idea is to have partners balance on their book together, without their feet touching the floor, without leaning against desk, walls, and so forth, and only using each other as support.
3. Have two groups go at a time, until everyone has *tried*. (Each group will not always succeed.)

## Suggestions for Discussion

How did you have fun?

What was the most important ingredient to succeed in this task? Why? (Or, for younger children: What did you have to do to succeed at this task?)

_____

_____

_____

_____

Charlene C. Wenc

Activity 13
# Camp Cooperative

## Purpose

To provide an opportunity for the group to plan and work cooperatively.

What they construct exemplifies how they worked together.

## Materials

Newspaper

Masking tape

## Procedure

1. Divide the class into groups of five.
2. Give each group a pile of newspapers and a roll of masking tape.
3. Tell them they are to make a shelter which they could camp in that's large enough to protect the entire group.
4. Give them a four-minute planning time for brainstorming ideas *before* touching the paper or tape.
5. Tell the group that every member must have a part in the entire activity.
6. Give them six or seven minutes to actually build the structure.

## Suggestions for Discussion

Give each group an opportunity to show the others what they constructed.

Ask them how they got their ideas.

Ask in what ways they are pleased with their structure. Did everyone have a part in it?

Activity 14
# Checkerboard

## Purpose
To provide an opportunity to work together for a common goal.

## Materials
Two sheets of construction paper (approximately 24" x 16"; two colors)

## Procedure
1. Divide the class into partners.
2. Hand each pair a set of paper.
3. Tell them that they are to make a checkerboard design together with the paper without using *any* equipment except the paper.
4. Tell them that they are *not to talk* to each other.
5. Set a time limit of five minutes.
6. Let everyone walk around to see what others accomplished.

## Suggestions for Discussion
How were you able to do this activity?

What did you learn about working together today?

Can you use this knowledge any other time at school?

_____

_____

_____

_____

Charlene C. Wenc

Activity 15
# Cooperative Strings

## Purpose

To allow the group to work together in a way that increases member's sensitivity to each other.

## Materials

Pieces of rope tied into a circle; one rope for each group

## Procedure

1. Divide the class into groups of five or six.
2. Each group is given a rope.
3. Tell the class that from this point there is *no talking.*
4. Each child is to keep both hands on the rope and together the group is to form the items that you say.
5. Say: Make the rope into:

   1. a circle
   2. a square            7. a butterfly
   3. a rectangle         8. a tree
   4. a pentagon          9. a flower
   5. a flag              10. a tall building
   6. a kite

6. You may move into affective items by telling the class to make the rope look: smiling, frowning, nervous, happy, friendly, angry, sad.

**Note:** You may use the rope to review map skills, other geometric figures, and so forth.

## Suggestions for Discussion

How were we able to get the rope to do what was asked?

How did it feel to cooperate and be part of the group?

When did we work together today in our class?

If everyone cooperates, how does that help you?

Activity 16
# Create a Masterpiece

## Purpose
Cooperation is an important part of working together.

## Materials
Poster-size paper taped to wall or chalkboard
Felt marker

## Procedure
1. Divide the class into three teams.
2. Each team is lined up in front of the paper.
3. The idea of the game is for each team to create a picture. To make it interesting, each person comes to the paper and adds only one of the following:

   a ◯ (circle) or four ‖‖‖ (straight lines). Each must

   build on what the preceding person has done.
4. Show an example such as:

5. Tell them this is not a race!
6. Repeat this activity with the *same* teams.

## Suggestions for Discussion
What great pictures! Show them to the class. Hang them up in the room if possible.

Did the picture turn out the way you expected? No? That sometimes happens in cooperation! *You aren't* always in control. Some people don't like that.

How did you cooperate in working together?

Activity 17

# Line Groups

## Purpose

To work together and to treat each other with respect.

## Materials

None

## Procedure

1. I am going to give you a number 1, 2, 3, 4. Please remember what number I gave you. (Walk around the room assigning numbers to each child.)
2. No. 4 — please come and quietly line up right here.
3. No. 3 — please come and quietly line up right here.
4. No. 2 — please come and quietly line up right here.
5. No. 1 — please come and quietly line up right here.
6. Separate the groups around the room.
7. In order to help us work as a group, we need to do this without talking.
8. First, make your line as long as you can. Comment—great job, good idea, and so forth.
9. Second, make your line as short as possible—Comment.
10. Third, make your line with the tallest person in the front and the shortest person in the back. Please do this without speaking.
11. Fourth, line up according to your birthday: January to December. Please do this without speaking.
12. Fifth, line up alphabetical order according to the first letter of your first name.

## Suggestions for Discussion

How did you do that so quickly? Was one person more important than the others?

You proved you can work well together. Congratulations!

How will working together help our group?

Activity 18

# Musical Laps

## Purpose

To demonstrate to the class that the idea of working together can help win a competitive activity.

## Materials

A record or tape of lively music

## Procedure

1. Tell the class to spread out, standing around the room.

2. This game is similar to musical chairs in that you find a place to sit as soon as the music stops. However, *there are no chairs!* When the music stops, you have a choice to make your lap into a chair for someone else by stooping, *or* to find a lap to sit in!

3. As the music stops, everyone must pair up. The last two people to pair up each time the music stops are out of the game. Let's see who is last to finish.

4. While the music is playing, everyone must keep moving. Ready! Go!

## Suggestions for Discussion

Did you have fun? Do you think cooperation is fun?

How did certain people manage to stay in the game?

Can you tell me how you had to work together during this activity?

　　　　　　　　　　　Charlene C. Wenc

Activity 19
# Rhythm Clapping

## Purpose

To emphasize the idea of working together and sharing leadership.

## Materials

None

## Procedure

1. Clap a particular rhythm and then point to the group to repeat it. Compliment the group on how well they are working together.
2. Now ask different children to do a clapping pattern for the group. (It is a good idea to select an obvious leader to do this the first time.)

## Suggestions for Discussion

How did you all clap so well together?

When did we have to work together today? How did that go compared with "Rhythm Clapping"? Any suggestions for improvement?

_____

_____

_____

_____

Activity 20

# Shuffle, Shuffle, Shuffle

## Purpose

To give experience in working together. To help the group to realize the power they have to solve problems.

## Materials

None

## Procedure

1. Can I have six volunteers to stand up here in a straight line next to me?. . . . Great!

2. Now, we'll look at you while you look at us. Class, please close your eyes now while we change our positions up front here.

3. Okay, open your eyes and take a look at us now. Your job is to put us back together in the same order in which we started out.

4. Each one of you can come up here and shift one of us to a different position in a line until we're all back together in our original positions. Who wants to begin?

(The leader will ask these questions and will do the shuffling of the line at number 3.)

## Suggestions for Discussion

Many of you wanted to be a part of this. That is great! We all like to be included.

How did you work together here?

How did you treat each other?

Did you have fun?

It feels good to be a part of something.

Charlene C. Wenc

Activity 21
# Snake Ball Pass

## Purpose

To enable the group to work together.

## Materials

Two soft balls

## Procedure

1. Tell the group we are going to see how fast we can pass one ball up and down the rows like a snake.

2. Begin with one person and time how fast it took to pass the ball to the last person.

3. Repeat the activity to see if the group can improve its speed.

4. Start the ball with the last person and reverse the passing. Time this procedure also.

5. If the group is working well, start two balls, one with the first person and one with the last person. Explain to the children the balls will pass in the middle of the group. The class loves this part. Time it and have fun!

## Suggestions for Discussion

Did we have to work together?

What made us faster?

How did we help each other?

Activity 22
# Up, Up and Away

## Purpose

To allow the class to experience working together and to ensure that everyone belongs.

## Materials

Three round party balloons

## Procedure

1. Tell the class they are going to have some fun working together keeping balloons in the air.
2. Have the children form a circle.
3. Tell them to be sure everyone has a turn.
4. Begin to pass a balloon around the group.

**Note:**   You may vary this activity as follows:

   a. Use three balloons, keeping them *all* in the air.
   b. Time how long the group can keep a balloon up before it lands on the floor.
   c. Change the group's location from a circle to rows or to being seated.

## Suggestions for Discussion

Did everyone have an opportunity for a turn?

Did you work to ensure that others had a change? Or—said with humor!—Were you more interested in your turn?

How did the group cooperate in this activity?

Can we cooperate this way at another time today? Can you think of occasions when we can do this?

Charlene C. Wenc

Activity 23

# Who is the Leader?

## Purpose

To demonstrate that cooperation makes working together in a group easy.

## Materials

None

## Procedure

1. You and the class form a circle.
2. One child is sent out of the room.
3. One child is assigned to be the leader.
4. The class is told to do exactly what the leader does.
5. The child is called back to the group to guess who the leader is. The child may have up to three guesses.

**Note:** Give the whole class a few minutes of following your actions *before* the actual game begins.

## Suggestions for Discussion

How were we able to move so well together?

Compliment the group on working so well together.

_____

_____

_____

_____

Charlene C. Wenc

# Part III
# Cooperation Builds
# a Positive Environment

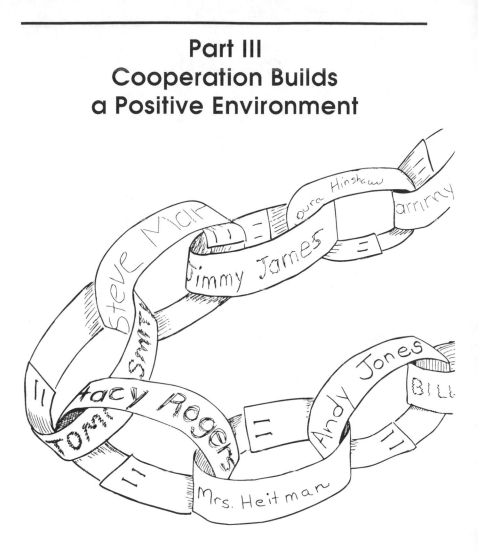

## Cooperative Chain

Activity 24

# Car Wash

## Purpose

To encourage positive interaction among the group by fostering awareness of cooperation.

## Materials

None

## Procedure

1. Have the children form two lines facing one another with a two-foot space between the lines.
2. Ask for one volunteer to stand at the start of the two lines.

EXAMPLE:    ----------------------------------------------------------

    Volunteer •

                     ----------------------------------------------------------

3. Tell the class that we are going to do a "car wash" without any water, brushes, or cars!
4. Ask the volunteer to walk down the "car wash" and tell each child to say something nice about him or her. You can say, "Now here is our first person to go through the car wash. I'll give you a minute to think of something nice to say."

## Note:

a. Do not do more than two at a time.

b. This activity can be repeated throughout the year. All children enjoy having a turn.

5. After the first person has gone through, comment on the shining smile that the group put on the volunteer's face with their compliments—no further discussion is needed!

Charlene C. Wenc

Activity 25
# Catch Them

## Purpose

To foster an awareness of the cooperative and helpful actions of others.

## Materials

Pin up a *large* sheet of paper with the title "CATCH THEM" at the top.

## Procedure

1. Tell the children you have seen a lot of helpful and cooperative acts in this class that you would like to record. Ask the children to help you with this project.

2. Tell them whenever they "catch" someone being cooperative or helpful, to come to the "Catch Them" chart, write the child's name down, and write down what they did in a brief way. Give some examples:

   Bobby shared a book with Eddie.

   Mary complimented Eve.

**Note:** You may make a collection of these for a bulletin board or a newsletter to parents.

## Suggestions for Discussion

At the end of the day, compliment the class on all the "Catch Them" actions listed.

Ask the class if they would like to do it again.

Activity 26
# Cooperative Chain

## Purpose

To remind the class that in a cooperative environment each plays an active part.

## Materials

Yellow strips of construction paper, 11" x 4"; one for each student and the teacher

A stapler

## Procedure

1. Give one strip to each person.
2. Tell the children to sign their names on one side of the strip.

> ### Susan

3. Collect them one at a time, stapling them in rings connected to each other.
4. Put the chain up in the room, explaining to the class that it is a symbol of cooperation in a class.

## Suggestions for Discussion

How could the chain be broken?

What can we do to keep it together?

How long do you think we can keep it together?

Shall we try for that time?

Charlene C. Wenc

Activity 27
# Face Pictures

## Purpose

To demonstrate that cooperation can be fun if everyone participates, and to learn that sharing is a part of cooperation.

## Materials

Drawing paper and one crayon for each child

## Procedure

1. Each child is asked to take out one crayon.
2. Give each child a piece of paper.
3. Ask the children to write their names on their papers, then to turn their papers over.
4. Tell the children to make a large circle or oval on the paper and pass the paper to the left.
5. Make a nose and pass the paper.
6. Make a mouth and pass it.
7. Make two eyes and pass it.
8. Make hair and pass it.
9. Make two ears and pass it back to the person whose name is on the back.

## Suggestions for Discussion

Give time for the children to react to their pictures and observe their behavior. Comment to the class that there was a lot of laughter and how many had fun. Note that some *aren't* happy about their pictures and ask why.

Discuss that sometimes in cooperation things don't work out the way we expect or want them to.

Ask the class if cooperation takes sharing. Is it easy to share all the time?

Activity 28
# Forced Choices

## Purpose

To introduce to the group the importance of everyone's need to belong.

## Materials

3 x 5 cards, masking tape, pens or markers

## Procedure

1. Handout one card to each person (leader plays also).
2. On the chalkboard, draw a large card and divide it into four sections.
3. Tell the group to write one choice in each box.
4. They must choose one item from each set.
5. They are not to share their choices with anyone else.
6. Ideas for choices are: chocolate or vanilla ice cream, cat or dog, California or Florida, Ferrari or Porsche, apple or blueberry pie, Coke or Seven Up.
7. Write down the choices. Please don't tell anyone your choices; it makes it more interesting.
8. Call the groups up to get tape.
9. Tape the card on so others can see what you chose.
10. Walk around and see if you can find people who have made the same choice as you (all four need to be the same).
11. Allow time for this; you mingle also.
12. Ask everyone to freeze and be quiet.
13. Ask who found someone who had the same choices as they did (attempt to help those who have not).

Charlene C. Wenc

**Suggestions for Discussion**

How did you feel when you found someone?

Did it depend on who it was?

What if you couldn't find anyone? How did it feel?

Some people change their choices. Why?

Give some examples of this.

- We make choices sometimes because of what others are doing.
- Sometimes this is OK. Other times it doesn't help us and gets us into trouble.

_____

_____

_____

_____

Activity 29
# Good at Pantomimes

## Purpose

To increase the positive attitude of group members toward each other.

## Materials

None

## Procedure

1. Tell the group members to think of something they are good at.
2. Ask them to volunteer to come to the front of the room one at a time to act these things out in pantomime. (It encourages others if you participate, too.)
3. The group tries to guess what each volunteer is acting out.
4. Encourage as many as possible to participate.

## Suggestions for Discussion

Tell the group it is important to know what we are good at, that this is not bragging, but sharing, and that we all have things we are proud to know how to do.

Activity 30
# Goodie Messages

## Purpose

To help build a positive environment for all the students.

## Materials

3 x 5 yellow cards; one for each student

## Procedure

1. Pass out one card to each.
2. Tell them to write their names on the cards, and then to fold the cards in half.
3. Collect the folded cards.
4. Pass these cards out to each child. (Make certain the children don't get their own cards.)
5. Tell the students to write down one *good* thing you know about that person. (Give a few examples.)
6. When they are finished, tell them to hand the cards back to you.
7. Return each card to the child whose name is on the card.

**Note:** Remind the students that only positive, kind things are to be written.

## Suggestions for Discussion

Why is this activity called "goodie messages?"

Did you feel good when you received your card back?

Is it important to share good things about each other?

Activity 31
# Pipe Cleaner Cooperative

## Purpose
To foster the ability of the group to cooperate *voluntarily*.

## Materials
Two pipe cleaners for each student

## Procedure
1. Give each child two pipe cleaners.
2. Tell them that when you say "Go," they can join together in groups of two, three, or four, or stay alone.
3. They may make anything they wish, working with their pipe cleaners or combining pipe cleaners.

## Suggestions for Discussion
Is it easier to work alone or together?

How much of your day do you spend alone? With others?

Charlene C. Wenc

Activity 32
# Secret Buddies

## Purpose

To create a supportive atmosphere in the group.

## Materials

3 x 5 index cards

## Procedure

1. Pass out a card to each student and yourself.
2. Have each child write his or her own name on the card, fold the card in half, and place it in a box or other container.
3. Tell the class we are having "secret buddy" assignments for the day. Tell them it will be each of our jobs to make the effort to be friendly and helpful to this one person for the rest of the day *without* letting anyone know who your "secret buddy" is. At the end of the day we will tell who the secret buddy is.
4. Ask the class for ideas for what a friendly, helpful buddy could do for you.
5. Let's keep our secret and enjoy our job!
6. Tell the children to come to the container one at a time, take out a card and read the name. That is their "secret buddy" for the day.

## Suggestions for Discussion

After sharing who our secret buddy was, ask for examples of what we did for them.

What was good about it?

What kind of a day did we have as a group?

Activity 33
# The Rottens

## Purpose
To stress the reality of an environment *without* cooperation.

## Materials
Drawing paper and box of crayons for each child

## Procedure
1. Ask the children to draw a picture about a school in a kingdom where no cooperation exists.
2. Tell the children to use their imaginations and to have fun.

**Note:** Pictures can be used as a bulletin board display.

## Suggestions for Discussion
Would people be happy in a school like this?
Would the children learn well?
What would be the worst part of going to school there?

_____

_____

_____

_____

Charlene C. Wenc

# Part IV
# Cooperation is
# Helpful to Everyone

## Candy Co-op

Activity 34

# Candy Co-op

## Purpose

To foster the idea that helping each other is an important part of cooperation.

## Materials

Individually wrapped candy (one piece for each child)

## Procedure

1. Explain to the class that he or she is going to hide a piece of candy for each one outside.

2. There are three rules to this game:

   a. You can only pick up *one* piece of candy.

   b. If you find another piece, you don't touch it; instead, you help someone else get it who doesn't have any.

   c. You don't eat the candy until everyone has a piece.

## Suggestions for Discussion

How did everyone find the candy?

Did you work together?

What could have happened if people hadn't cooperated?

Why is cooperation better for the whole group?

Activity 35

# Cooperative Squares

## Purpose

To assess the level of cooperation in the group and to stress that cooperation is helpful to everyone.

## Materials

A. Cut the shapes shown below from five six-inch squares of tag board:

B. Place the pieces into five envelopes in these combinations:

     Envelope 1—Pieces I, H, E

     Envelope 2—Pieces A, A, A, C

     Envelope 3—Pieces A, J

     Envelope 4—Pieces D, F

     Envelope 5—Pieces G, B, F, C

## Procedure

1. Divide the class into five groups.
2. Tell the class each group will be given one envelope containing pieces to make squares.
3. The job of the class is to form five equal six-inch squares.
4. There are two rules:
   a. No talking.
   b. You may not take a piece away from someone else. You may only give away your own pieces and take the pieces which are offered to you.

## Suggestions for Discussion

Was the game difficult? How were you able to make the squares? Did everyone in your group help? What could your group do next time to improve this activity?

This activity is from the *DUSO II Kit* by Don C. Dinkmeyer, Sr. Circle Pines, MN: American Guidance Services, 1973. Adapted by permission of the publisher.

Charlene C. Wenc

Activity 36
# "Fuzzy" Co-op

## Purpose

To develop the positive in the group by experiencing that it is easier to work together when we realize the people around us appreciate our good qualities.

## Materials

Two soft balls (any size)

## Procedure

1. Form two circles.
2. Give one ball to each circle.
3. Tell the class we are going to pass the ball to those on our right, and that *as* we pass it to them, we are to say something nice about them.
4. Now pass the ball to the *left*, and say something nice about those on your left.

## Suggestions for Discussion

Thank the class and tell them that people can realize many good things about each other and themselves when they are members of a group.

Do you like to work with someone who you think does not like you? Why not?

Activity 37
# Go There

## Purpose

To demonstrate what happens when each member of a group insists on having his or her own way.

## Materials

None

## Procedure

1. Have the entire class form a circle, including you.
2. Tell the class to look around the room carefully.
3. Now tell them to shut their eyes and think of a place in the room they would like to go to.
4. Ask them to open their eyes and hold hands.
5. Tell them they are each to move toward their chosen place *without letting go of hands.*
6. After *a few seconds,* tell the group to freeze and to notice where they are.
7. Tell them to let go of their hands and return to their seats.

## Suggestions for Discussion

Did anyone get where he or she wanted to go?

How many here like to have things their own way?

Some group members get their own way often. What can we do to encourage them to cooperate?

Charlene C. Wenc

Activity 38

# How Do You Measure Up?

## Purpose

To allow students to cooperate with a partner in a helping manner; to share, take turns, and speak to each other in a kind way.

## Materials

Two pieces of masking tape per student

## Procedure

1. Tell the children to find someone whose thumb is the same size as theirs. (This is a good way to choose partners!)
2. Explain that they are going to do some estimating today and they are going to help each other.
3. Demonstrate how to do the activity with one of the students and yourself:

   Say, "I am going to guess how tall I am by putting two pieces of tape on the floor, one where I think my head would be and one where my feet would be. Then I will lie down between the two points and my partner will tell me if I am right or wrong and help me if I need it. We will take turns."

4. Have the class measure height. (Vary the activity by estimating the length of their arms, feet, legs.)

**Note:** This activity is great for the loners in your class to feel included in a non-threatening way.

## Suggestions for Discussion

Were you helpful to your partner? How?

Were you polite and kind?

Were you surprised by your own measurements?

Did you think you were shorter or taller?

_____

_____

_____

_____

Activity 39

# Name Relay

## Purpose

To show that in competition a group must cooperate, and to teach the value of sportsmanship.

## Materials

Chalkboard

Chalk

## Procedure

1. Divide class into two groups.
2. Line up the groups in front of the board in relay order.
3. Tell them this is a relay race. The first person to the board writes his or her full first name, then passes the chalk to the next person to do so, and goes to the end of the line. The second time at the board, they write their *last* names. The idea is to see which team finishes first.

## Suggestions for Discussion

It is always fun to comment on their "lovely" handwriting when it is over and to share a laugh about it.

How did cooperation exist in this game? How did it help?

How did you treat each other in the winning? The losing?

Activity 40
# Paper Charades

## Purpose
To allow each person to belong and have value in the group.

## Materials
8 x 10 paper or chalkboard, pencil or chalk

## Procedure
1. Tell the class this is a race playing "charades" using the paper to describe items instead of pantomime.
2. Give the class an example. Show the card with "tree" on it, and draw a tree on the board. As soon as they recognize the object, let them call out the answer (or raise a hand to be called on).
3. Divide the class into teams of four people.
4. Give each team a marker and paper. Select one person to be the starter.
5. The teacher shows a card to each individual as he or she comes to the head of the team's line, without letting other team members see the card.
6. Each child draws the item on the paper. As soon as the team guesses what the item is, it is the next child's turn.
7. Call time after 5 to 6 minutes.

## Suggestions for Discussion
Did you have fun?

How was cooperation a part of the game?

How did cooperation help your team?

Activity 41
# Pennies on a Book

## Purpose

To show that cooperation is difficult at times because it means we have to consider other people.

## Materials

A telephone book with a penny on each corner

## Procedure

1. Tell two children to stand on the book.
2. Working together, they are to pick up the pennies *without* stepping off the book.

**Note:** This is an opportunity to pair popular children with the isolates in your class.

## Suggestions for Discussion

What did it take to pick up the pennies? Why were some people successful so quickly? Did this activity take planning? Does cooperation take planning? When in this activity did you plan?

Activity 42
# Robot Control

## Purpose

To experience relying on someone else in order to demonstrate that cooperation is easier with trust, and to emphasize that we all gain or lose depending on the degree of our cooperation.

## Materials

None

## Procedure

1. Divide the class into partners.
2. Tell them to decide who will be A and B.
3. Ask if they can all show how a robot moves around. Good!
4. Tell them that B will be the controller of the robot while A will be the robot. It is B's job to direct A around the room so that the robot does not bump into anything or anyone. Ready? Go!
5. Let them move around for a few minutes and then tell them to stop and switch, so that A is now the controller and B is the robot.

## Suggestions for Discussion

Let's talk about what happened. Why is trust important in a group?

Is it better when we trust only a few people, or when we trust everyone in our group?

Charlene C. Wenc

**Stringing Along**

 Charlene C. Wenc

Activity 43

# Stringing Along

## Purpose

To emphasize that *sharing* is an important part of cooperation. Sharing may entail giving up your own way in order to blend your ideas with others, an ability you need now and will need in the future.

## Materials

One four-foot length of string for each group

Piece of masking tape or roll of tape for each child

## Procedure

1. Divide the class into groups of four or five children each.
2. Have the group members stand together.
3. Distribute one string and pieces of tape to each group.
4. Tell the groups you want them to make a $\Delta$ with the string and tape it down to the floor.
5. Have the members close their eyes. Now tell them to kneel down and, *with eyes closed,* make a $\Delta$ .
6. Do the same activity, but this time have the group make a circle on the floor.

## Suggestions for Discussion

Discuss with the group what they observed.

How would you improve your group?

Activity 44
# Toothpick Pictures

## Purpose

To train a group to be helpful and work together. To allow others to share.

## Materials

Boxes of toothpicks

## Procedures

1. Have the students work in pairs the first time you do this activity. Give each pair a pile of about 50 toothpicks.

2. The task is for the children to make some kind of creation from their toothpicks. Anything is acceptable—a design, a picture, a sculpture—whatever they can come up with. The only ground rules are that each person get a chance to help decide what the creation will be and that each person get a chance to help make it.

3. After fifteen minutes or so, have everyone stop. Give the class a chance to wander around the room and see what everyone has made.

4. Repeat this activity a number of times. Each time increase the number of students in the group.

**Note:**   Procedure number 4 is optional.

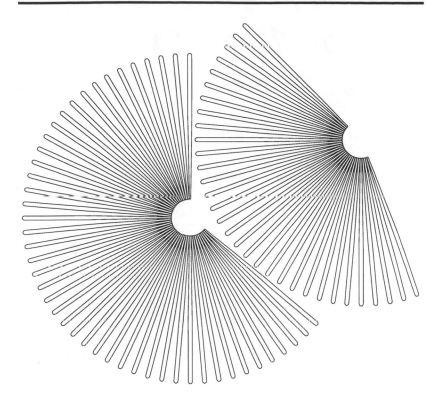

## Suggestions for Discussion

How did you decide what to make?
What problems did you encounter in deciding?
How did you solve them?
What problems did you have with the materials?
How did you solve them?

NOTES

# Part V
# Cooperation is Powerful

**Cooperative Lift**

Activity 45
# Brainstorming

## Purpose

Groups enjoy this experience—members are proud of the number of things they can think of together. Teachers can use this success as a catalyst in the classroom.

## Materials

Three objects (e.g., plastic cup, yardstick, scarf or other piece of fabric)

## Procedure

1. The class is asked to define *brainstorming*.

2. Once this is established, ask the class who they think could come up with more uses for the plastic cup: a person working alone or a group of people? (In most cases, the majority of students will feel that *one* person will, because one person would *really* try, while the group may become noisy and not work as hard at it.)

3. Choose one child to leave the classroom with a paper and pencil to brainstorm all the uses he or she can for a plastic cup, and to make a list of these ideas.

4. While the child is gone, ask the rest of the class to brainstorm uses for the plastic cup together, while you write their ideas on the board.

5. After four to five minutes, call the child back. While he or she is at the door, ask how many uses are on the child's list, then invite the child to rejoin the group.

6. Continue brainstorming with the group with the other objects.

## Suggestions for Discussion

Discuss with the class what happened and how they felt about it.

Acknowledge contributions and good ideas, efforts made by all, and the group's success.

Charlene C. Wenc

Activity 46
# Chalkboard Charade Relay

## Purpose

To emphasize that even in competition, cooperation is important.

## Materials

3 x 5 index cards with an item listed on each one (e.g., tree, car, bike, chair, cup, elephant)

## Procedure

1. Tell the class this is a race playing "charades," using the chalkboard to describe items instead of pantomime.
2. Give the class an example. Show the card with "tree" on it, and draw a tree on the board. As soon as they recognize the object, let them call out the answer (or raise a hand to be called on).
3. Divide the class into two teams.
4. Line up each team, relay style, in front of a panel of the chalkboard with a piece of chalk and an eraser.
5. Show a card to each individual as he or she comes to the head of the team's line, without letting other team members see the card.
6. Each child draws the item on the board. As soon as the team guesses what the item is, it is the next child's turn.
7. First team finished wins.

## Suggestions for Discussion

Did you have fun?

How was cooperation a part of the game?

How did cooperation help your team?

Activity 47
# Co-op Alphabet

## Purpose

To brainstorm different aspects of cooperation with the class.

## Materials

Chalkboard

Chalk

## Procedure

1. On the chalkboard, write the alphabet.

    A. _____

    B. _____

    C. _____

2. Tell the children we are going to write as many words as possible to fill in our alphabet with words that relate to cooperation.

3. Time limit: ten to fifteen minutes

## Suggestions for Discussion

Encourage the class by telling them what a good job they did. Comment that cooperation was necessary to do the project.

See if one or more class members would like to copy and display the "Co-op Alphabet."

Activity 48
# Cooperative Lift

## Purpose

To stress the power of cooperation.

## Materials

One classroom chair

## Procedure

1. The children are told that they are going to lift a child off a chair just by using their fingers.

2. Ask the children if they think they can lift the child off the chair. Ask five of those who believe it *can* be done to participate in the activity.

3. One child is chosen to sit in the chair.

4. The four others stand near the child, two at the shoulders and two at the knees.

5. The four are told that their task will be to make a fist of each hand, leaving their index fingers sticking straight out, and to lift the child under the armpits and knees.

6. The rest of the class is asked to help by counting together from one to ten and saying "Lift!"

7. On the counts of one to eight, each of the four children lays hands, one on top of the other at each count, on the head of the child in the chair. At the count of nine, they make their fists and stick out their index fingers. At the count of ten, they position their fingers under each armpit and each knee. And then they are told "LIFT!"

**Note:** A practice or two is necessary before they *actually* lift so that the timing is right.

**Suggestions for Discussion**

How were you able to do it?

How did it feel?

Who else would like to do it? Why?

What makes cooperation so powerful?

This activity is from *Redirecting Children's Misbehavior*, by Kathy and Bill Kvols-Riedler. Boulder, CO: RDIC Publications, 1981. Adapted by permission of the publisher.

Activity 49
# Cooperative Tray

## Purpose

To stress to students that they can accomplish more in a group than by themselves.

## Materials

A large tray filled with ten to twelve objects (e.g., pencil, scissors, flower, key, coin, bank, cap, rock, fork, stuffed animal, notebook, jewelry), and a cloth to cover the tray

## Procedure

1. Tell the class to clear their desks.
2. Take the tray around, shows it to the children, and ask them to remember as many items as they can. Cover the tray between "viewings."
3. Divide the class into partners and ask the pairs to write down on a sheet of paper the objects they recall.

## Suggestions for Discussion

How did you help each other?

Name one kind thing your partner said to you.

Tell the class that people can usually get a lot accomplished in a cooperative group.

Activity 50
# List of Feelings

## Purpose
To demonstrate that a group can accomplish more than one person can.

## Materials
A roll of paper (like a scroll)

## Procedure
1. Ask the class to think about words that describe feelings.
2. Tell them that one class listed 96 feeling words. Can we do that many? Let's try!
3. Ask them to tell you their words. Write the words down on the scroll. After about ten minutes tell the children they are doing wonderfully, and that if they can think of other words during the day they are to add them to the list quietly. We'll see how many we have at the end of the day. (It is important that you add to the list also.)
4. At the end of the day proudly display what was done, and stress what can be done together.

**Note:** This "list idea" can be used in Language Arts for making lists of parts of speech; in Math, for math concepts; in Social Studies, for lists of resources; in Science, for classification, and so forth.

## Suggestions for Discussion
How do you feel about our list?

Congratulations to all of us!

Let's clap for us!

Activity 51
# Transformation Stick

## Purpose

Cooperation shows the power of our intelligence as we work together.

## Materials

Ruler or yardstick

## Procedure

The group sits in a circle as the leader holds a stick about three feet long. The leader gets up and moves across the circle showing what the stick has become (a cane, a gun, a paddle, a bat, a rope, a broom, a horse, a leash with a tiger on the end, and so forth). The leader gives the stick to the person directly opposite him or her in the circle. The new leader gets up, taking the stick as given and, as he or she moves across the circle, transforms the stick into a new thing, handing on the new thing to the next person to the right of the old leader. And so the stick passes back and forth across the circle, being transformed as it goes. Each new leader must concentrate on taking the stick as given and then transforming it (not merely taking it and changing it) as he or she moves across the circle. Other simple objects such as a ball, a hoop, or a short piece of rope can be used in place of the stick. For more advanced groups, volunteers can come to the center and take the stick from the leader, so that the action takes place in the center rather than passing across the circle.

**Note:**   You can allow students to stay at their desks and pass it to them. It creates less confusion.

## Suggestions for Discussion

How were you able to get that many?

If we were all the same, would we have so many ideas?

Is it helpful to be different?

# References

Dewey, E.A. (1978). *Basic applications of Adlerian psychology.* Coral Springs, FL: CMTI Press.

Dinkmeyer, D.C. (1973). *DUSO II kit.* Circle Pines, MN: American Guidance Services.

Foster, E.S. (1989). *Energizers and icebreakers: For all ages and stages.* Minneapolis, MN: Educational Media Corporation.

Kvois-Riedler, K. and Kvois-Riedler, B. (1981) Reducing children's misbehavior. Boulder, CO: RDIC Publications.

**Office of Counseling,
Career and
Learning Support Services
Walker Hall 124**